YOU'RE NOT
OLD
YOU'RE JUST
NOT THAT YOUNG

HARVEY LITTLE

summersdale

YOU'RE NOT OLD, YOU'RE JUST NOT THAT YOUNG

Summersdale Publishers Ltd
46 West Street
Chichester
West Sussex
PO19 1RP
UK

www.summersdale.com

Printed and bound in India by Nutech Print Services

ISBN: 978-1-84953-328-7

Substantial discounts on bulk quantities of Summersdale books are available to corporations, professional associations and other organisations. For details contact Summersdale Publishers by telephone: +44 (0) 1243 771107, fax: +44 (0) 1243 786300 or email: nicky@summersdale.com.

TO..

FROM..

CONTENTS

CONTENTS

THE BRIGHT SIDE

WHATEVER WITH THE PAST HAS GONE, THE BEST IS ALWAYS YET TO COME.

Lucy Larcom

I'm happy to report that my
inner child is still ageless.

James Broughton

Youth is the gift of nature,
but age is a work of art.

Garson Kanin

I can still rock like a son of a bitch.

Ozzy Osbourne

Just remember, once
you're over the hill, you
begin to pick up speed.

Charles M. Schulz

First you are young; then you
are middle-aged; then you are
old; then you are wonderful.

Diana Cooper

A comfortable old age is the
reward of a well-spent youth.

Maurice Chevalier

FASCINATING FACT

Proof that you can do what you love well into old age is Adam Kelly, Britain's oldest ice cream man. He celebrated his 90th birthday by doing what he does six days of the week – selling ice cream!

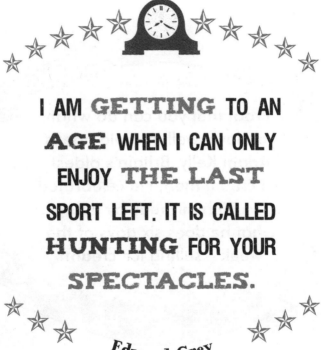

I AM **GETTING** TO AN
AGE WHEN I CAN ONLY
ENJOY **THE LAST**
SPORT LEFT. IT IS CALLED
HUNTING FOR YOUR
SPECTACLES.

Edward Grey

Autumn is really the best of the seasons; and I'm not sure that old age isn't the best part of life.

C. S. Lewis

You only live once, but if you do it right, once is enough.

Mae West

To be 70 years young is sometimes far more cheerful and hopeful than to be 40 years old.

Oliver Wendell Holmes Jr

Men are like wine. Some
turn to vinegar, but the
best improve with age.

Pope John XXIII

Our wrinkles are our medals
of the passage of life. They are
what we have been through...

Lauren Hutton

Old age likes indecency.
It's a sign of life.

Mason Cooley

Youth is for freedom and reform, maturity for judicious compromise, and old age for stability and repose.

Winston Churchill

When you become senile, you won't know it.

Bill Cosby

Please don't retouch my wrinkles. It took me so long to earn them.

Anna Magnani

SEX IN THE SIXTIES
IS GREAT, BUT
IMPROVES IF YOU PULL
OVER TO THE SIDE
OF THE ROAD.

Johnny Carson

You'll lose your mind when you grow older. What they don't tell you is that you won't miss it very much.

Malcolm Cowley

Old age is an excellent time for outrage. My goal is to say or do at least one outrageous thing every week.

Maggie Kuhn

Perhaps one has to be very old before one learns to be amused rather than shocked.

Pearl S. Buck

Not a shred of evidence
exists in favour of the idea
that life is serious.

Brendan Gill

My grandmother is over 80
and still doesn't need glasses.
Drinks right out of the bottle.

Henny Youngman

Youth is the time for adventures
of the body, but age for the
triumphs of the mind.

Logan Pearsall Smith

FASCINATING FACT

It seems that there's some truth in the old adage 'age is just a number'. A survey conducted in 2011 showed that citizens of Greece believe that old age arrives when you turn 68, which presumably means that you can class yourself as a 'youngster' right up until then!

THE OLDER WE GET, THE BETTER WE USED TO BE.

John McEnroe

... long after wearing bifocals
and hearing aids, we'll still
be making love. We just
won't know with whom.

Jack Paar

My grandmother is 92 years
old and she hasn't a single
grey hair. She's bald.

Bernard Manning

I truly believe that age – if you're
healthy – is just a number.

Hugh Hefner

To be 70 years old is like climbing the Alps. You reach a snow-crowned summit, and see behind you the deep valley stretching miles...

Henry Wadsworth Longfellow

Age is never so old as youth would measure it.

Jack London

When grace is joined with wrinkles, it is adorable. There is an unspeakable dawn in happy old age.

Victor Hugo

FASCINATING FACT

A survey conducted in 2008 showed that many people grow happier as they grow older – up until the age of 50 life is more likely to feel troublesome, after which we start forgetting our worries and enjoying ourselves!

LAUGHTER DOESN'T REQUIRE TEETH.

Bill Newton

One man in his time
plays many parts.

William Shakespeare

Well, I suppose I must attribute it
to the fact that I haven't died yet.

Malcolm Sargent on being
asked to what he attributed
his advanced age of 70

As for me, except for an
occasional heart attack, I feel
as young as I ever did.

Robert Benchley

I think that's what makes life interesting – the evolution of getting older, and it's kinda fascinating...

Alexis Bledel

The older you get, the better you get – unless you're a banana.

Ross Noble

I'm kind of comfortable with getting older because it's better than the other option... so I'll take getting older.

George Clooney

FASCINATING FACT

Research in 2009 showed that the average 50-year-old is in better shape than a person half their age. At 50, a typical person will have a lower daily calorie intake and participate in a broader range of physical activities than an average 25-year-old.

KICKING BACK

Ten men waiting for me
at the door? Send one of
them home, I'm tired.

Mae West

When men reach their sixties
and retire, they go to pieces.
Women go right on cooking.

Gail Sheehy

It is necessary to relax your
muscles when you can.
Relaxing your brain is fatal.

Stirling Moss

I **ALWAYS** WAKE UP AT
THE **CRACK** OF ICE.

Joe E. Lewis

Old men should have more care
to end life well than to live long.

Anita Brookner

It is true you are gently
shouldered off the stage, but then
you are given such a comfortable
front stall as spectator.

Confucius on old age

The golden age is before
us, not behind us.

William Shakespeare

Live each day as if it were
your last, and garden as
though you will live forever.

Anonymous

If you associate enough
with older people who enjoy
their lives, you will gain the
possibility for a full life.

Margaret Mead

Retirement at 65 is ridiculous.
When I was 65 I still had pimples.

George Burns

FASCINATING FACT

The chilled-out art of t'ai chi has been shown to improve the health of older people. The gentle form of exercise improves breathing, relaxation and overall well-being – so there's really no need to bust a gut to stay fit!

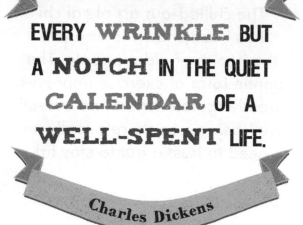

EVERY **WRINKLE** BUT A **NOTCH** IN THE QUIET **CALENDAR** OF A **WELL-SPENT** LIFE.

Charles Dickens

You can't turn back the clock.
But you can wind it up again.

Bonnie Prudden

Life has got to be lived.
That's all there is to it.

Eleanor Roosevelt

For us elderly people, not
owning a computer is like
not having a headache.

Edward Enfield

My crown is called content, a crown that seldom kings enjoy.

William Shakespeare

If you enjoy living, it is not difficult to keep the sense of wonder.

Ray Bradbury

A man has reached middle age when he is warned to slow down by his doctor rather than the police.

Henny Youngman

When a man retires his wife
gets twice the husband but
only half the income.

Chi Chi Rodriguez

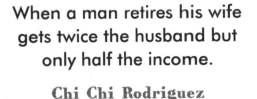

People are always asking about
the good old days. I say, why
don't you say the good now days?

Robert M. Young

Jameson's Irish Whiskey really
does improve with age: the
older I get the more I like it.

Bob Monkhouse

HOUSEWORK CAN'T
KILL YOU, BUT WHY
TAKE A CHANCE?

Phyllis Diller

Do not worry about avoiding
temptation. As you grow
older it will avoid you.

Joey Adams

A man is not old as long as
he is seeking something.

Jean Rostand

Life is too short to learn German.

Richard Porson

Every morning, like clockwork,
at 7 a.m., I pee. Unfortunately,
I don't wake up till 8.

Harry Beckworth

Do I exercise? Well I once
jogged to the ashtray.

Will Self

I think all old folks' homes should
have striptease. If I ran one I'd
have a striptease every week.

Cynthia Payne

FASCINATING FACT

Most would agree that a little doze does a lot of good. In support of this, statistics have shown that men and women who nap at least three times a week have a 37 per cent lower coronary mortality rate than those who don't.

THE **FIRST SIGN** OF **MATURITY** IS THE **DISCOVERY** THAT THE **VOLUME KNOB** ALSO **TURNS** TO THE LEFT.

Jerry M. Wright

Middle age is having a choice
between two temptations
and choosing the one that'll
get you home earlier.

Dan Bennett

I always make a point of
starting the day at 6 a.m. with
champagne. It goes straight to
the heart and cheers one up.

John Mortimer

My idea of a good night
out is a good night in.

Jack Rosenthal

At my age I do what Mark Twain did. I get my daily paper, look at the obituaries page and if I'm not there I carry on as usual.

Patrick Moore

A little nonsense now and then, is cherished by the wisest men.

Roald Dahl

The good thing about getting older is... you have less desire to go out and conquer everyone you see.

Julian Clary

FASCINATING FACT

It seems that laughter really is the best medicine. The simple act of laughing has been shown to have considerable health benefits for young and old, as the physical actions involved help to decrease stress, increase pain tolerance and, of course, reduce depression!

I **DON'T** WANT TO **RETIRE**. I'M **NOT** THAT **GOOD** AT **CROSSWORD** PUZZLES.

Norman Mailer

Cherish all your happy
moments; they make a fine
cushion for old age.

Booth Tarkington

Older people shouldn't eat
health food, they need all the
preservatives they can get.

Robert Orben

Sometimes I sits and thinks,
and sometimes I just sits.

Satchel Paige

A massage is just like a movie...
except in a massage you're
the star. And you don't miss
anything by falling asleep!

Elizabeth Jane Howard

How beautiful it is to do nothing
and then to rest afterward.

Spanish proverb

Since people are going to
be living longer and getting
older, they'll just have to learn
how to be babies longer.

Andy Warhol

FASCINATING FACT

You're never too old to rock 'n' roll! One in five festival goers in Britain are over 50, helped perhaps by the amount of over-fifties festivals held around the country.

BIRTHDAY BLUES

A diplomat is a man who always remembers a woman's birthday but never remembers her age.

Robert Frost

For all the advances in medicine, there is still no cure for the common birthday.

John Glenn

There is absolutely nothing to be said in favour of growing old. There ought to be legislation against it.

Patrick Moore

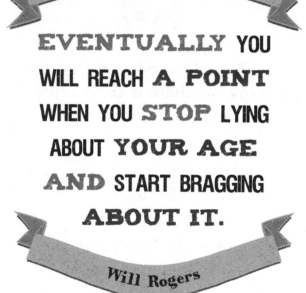

EVENTUALLY YOU
WILL REACH A POINT
WHEN YOU STOP LYING
ABOUT YOUR AGE
AND START BRAGGING
ABOUT IT.

Will Rogers

Oh, to be 70 again.

Georges Clemenceau on seeing a
pretty girl on his 80th birthday

I want to live to be 80 so I
can piss more people off.

Charles Bukowski

The years that a woman subtracts
from her age are not lost. They
are added to other women's.

Diane de Poitiers

Middle age is when you've met so many people that every new person you meet reminds you of someone else.

Ogden Nash

Why is a birthday cake the only food you can blow on... and everybody rushes to get a piece?

Bobby Kelton

My wife hasn't had a birthday in four years. She was born in the year of Lord-only-knows.

Anonymous

FASCINATING FACT

For her 102nd birthday Bess
Tancrelle realised her dream
of riding a Harley-Davidson
motorcycle, along with her
97-year-old sister in the sidecar.
On the back of her helmet
she placed a sticker with the
message, 'Screw it, let's ride.'

THERE ARE 364 DAYS
WHEN YOU MIGHT
GET UN-BIRTHDAY
PRESENTS... AND ONLY
ONE FOR BIRTHDAY
PRESENTS, YOU KNOW.

Lewis Carroll

We know we're getting old
when the only thing we
want for our birthday is not
to be reminded of it.

Anonymous

No woman should ever be
quite accurate about her age.
It looks so calculating.

Oscar Wilde

Last week the candle factory
burned down. Everyone
just stood around and
sang 'Happy Birthday'.

Steven Wright

Old age is always 15
years older than I am.

Oliver Wendell Holmes Sr

I'm not interested in age. People
who tell me their age are silly.
You're as old as you feel.

Elizabeth Arden

Every year on your birthday,
you get a chance to start new.

Sammy Hagar

Never worry about your
heart till it stops beating.

E. B. White

You can't stop the ageing
process. There's only so much
oil you can put on your body.

Angie Dickinson

Age is just a number. It's totally
irrelevant unless, of course, you
happen to be a bottle of wine.

Joan Collins

I JUST **TELL PEOPLE**
I'M **AS OLD** AS MY
WIFE. THEN **I LIE**
ABOUT HER AGE.

Fred Metcalf

A woman has the right to treat the subject of her age with ambiguity.

Helena Rubinstein

Let us celebrate the occasion with wine and sweet words.

Plautus

Birthdays are nature's way of telling us to eat more cake.

Anonymous

I believe in loyalty. When a woman reaches an age she likes she should stick to it.

Eva Gabor

It is so comic to hear oneself called old, even at 90 I suppose!

Alice James

The best birthdays are all those that haven't arrived yet.

Robert Orben

FASCINATING FACT

Apparently determined to party away the birthday blues, the Sultan of Brunei's 50th birthday party cost a whopping $27.2 million (£17.4 million) and included three concerts, one featuring Michael Jackson. That's enough to make the average birthday celebration seem like the bargain of the year!

AGE AIN'T NOTHING
BUT A NUMBER,
SO I FEEL GOOD.

Denzel Washington

The key to successful ageing
is to pay as little attention
to it as possible.

Judith Regan

There is only one cure for
grey hair. It was invented
by a Frenchman. It is
called the guillotine.

P. G. Wodehouse

I found my first grey hair
today. On my chest.

Wendy Liebman

The older I get, the older old is.

Tom Baker

As the talk turns to old age,
I say I am 49 plus VAT.

Lionel Blair

Age seldom arrives smoothly
or quickly. It's more often
a succession of jerks.

Jean Rhys

FASCINATING FACT

Floyd Creekmore, working under the name Creeky, was recognised as the oldest working clown in February 2012 at 95 years of age. An added bonus of being a clown, of course, is that he wouldn't have to pay out for any entertainment on his birthday!

BIRTHDAYS ARE GOOD FOR YOU. STATISTICS SHOW THAT THE PEOPLE WHO HAVE THE MOST LIVE THE LONGEST.

Larry Lorenzoni

Our birthdays are feathers
in the broad wing of time.

Jean Paul Richter

There is more felicity on the far
side of baldness than young
men can possibly imagine.

Logan Pearsall Smith

As a young man, I used to
have four supple members
and a stiff one. Now I have
four stiff and one supple.

Henri Duc D'Aumale

When you're 50, you start
thinking about things you
haven't thought about before...
Getting wrinkles is trivial.

Eugene O'Neill

I married an archaeologist
because the older I grow, the
more he appreciates me.

Agatha Christie

There is no cure for birth and
death, save to enjoy the interval.

George Santayana

FASCINATING FACT

By the time they reach 60, 3 in 5 men and 2 in 5 women will be snorers. So think twice the next time you get the urge to wedge a sock up your partner's nose when they're shaking the windows with their snoring!

GETTING PHYSICAL

After 30, a body has a
mind of its own.

Bette Midler

Life expectancy would grow
by leaps and bounds if
green vegetables smelled
as good as bacon.

Doug Larson

A man's health can be judged
by which he takes two at
a time – pills or stairs.

Joan Welsh

I REALLY **DON'T** THINK I
NEED BUNS OF STEEL. I'D
BE **HAPPY** WITH BUNS
OF **CINNAMON.**

Ellen DeGeneres

Advanced old age is when
you sit in a rocking chair
and can't get it going.

Eliakim Katz

The trouble with always trying to
preserve the health of the body is
that it is so difficult to do without
destroying the health of the mind.

G. K. Chesterton

I'm in pretty good shape
for the shape I'm in.

Mickey Rooney at 58

The need of exercise is a modern superstition, invented by people who ate too much, and had nothing to think about.

George Santayana

I wish I had the energy that my grandchildren have – if only for self-defence.

Gene Perret

I still have a full deck; I just shuffle slower now.

Anonymous

FASCINATING FACT

At 75, Ernestine Shepherd is the world's oldest competitive female bodybuilder and holds a Guinness World Record to prove it. She gets up at 3.00 a.m. to start her day of training, which involves working out, lifting weights and a 10-mile run!

BETWEEN **TWO EVILS,**
I **ALWAYS** PICK THE ONE
I NEVER **TRIED** BEFORE.

Mae West

Fitness – if it came in a
bottle, everybody would
have a great body.

Cher

My idea of exercise is
a good brisk sit.

Phyllis Diller

There's lots of people in this
world who spend so much time
watching their health that they
haven't the time to enjoy it.

Josh Billings

As you get older, the pickings get slimmer, but the people don't.

Carrie Fisher

Time is a dressmaker specialising in alterations.

Faith Baldwin

My doctor told me to do something that puts me out of breath, so I've taken up smoking again.

Jo Brand

NO **COWBOY** WAS
EVER FASTER ON **THE**
DRAW THAN A
GRANDPARENT
PULLING A **BABY**
PICTURE OUT OF
A **WALLET.**

Anonymous

The first time I see a jogger
smiling, I'll consider it.

Joan Rivers

Men chase golf balls when they're
too old to chase anything else.

Groucho Marx

To win back my youth... there is
nothing I wouldn't do – except
take exercise, get up early, or be a
useful member of the community.

Oscar Wilde

They say that age is all in your mind. The trick is keeping it from creeping down into your body.

Anonymous

As you get older three things happen. The first is your memory goes, and I can't remember the other two...

Norman Wisdom

Better to hunt in fields, for health unbought,
Than fee the doctor for a nauseous draught.

John Dryden

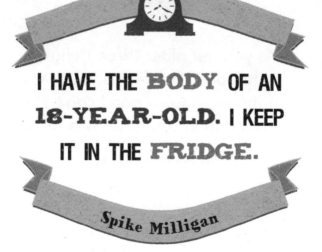

I HAVE THE **BODY** OF AN 18-YEAR-OLD. I KEEP IT IN THE **FRIDGE.**

Spike Milligan

You know you've reached middle-age when your weightlifting consists merely of standing up.

Bob Hope

My doctor says I should... get more fresh air and exercise. I said, 'All right, I'll drive with the car window open.'

Angus Walker

I knew I was going bald when it was taking me longer and longer to wash my face.

Harry Hill

I'm at an age when my back
goes out more than I do.

Phyllis Diller

I am pushing 60. That is
enough exercise for me.

Mark Twain

Exercise daily. Eat
wisely. Die anyway.

Anonymous

FASCINATING FACT

Swimming and cycling are two activities recommended for those who are getting on a bit. The advantage of both of these forms of exercise is that they don't put undue pressure on the joints. If you're not so good at swimming, there's always the shallow end – and no one ever forgets how to ride a bike!

FIBROIDS - ISN'T THAT A BREAKFAST CEREAL?

Victoria Wood

My mother is no spring chicken although she has got as many chemicals in her as one.

Barry Humphries (Dame Edna Everage)

Interviewer: Can you remember any of your past lives?

The Dalai Lama: At my age I have a problem remembering what happened yesterday.

I'd like to learn to ski but I'm 44 and I'm worried about my knees. They creak a lot and I'm afraid they might start an avalanche.

Jonathan Ross

And in the end it's not the years in your life that count. It's the life in your years.

Abraham Lincoln

Whenever I feel like exercise, I lie down until the feeling passes.

Robert M. Hutchins

Someone asked someone who was about my age: 'How are you?' The answer was, 'Fine. If you don't ask for details.'

Katharine Hepburn

FASCINATING FACT

Fauja Singh, the Turbaned
Tornado, believed to be the
world's oldest marathon runner,
ran his first marathon (London)
at the age of 89 in 2000, and at
the age of 101, ran what he has
said will be his last marathon
(also London) in 2012.

I **DARE** A LITTLE MORE
AS I GET **OLDER.**

Michel de Montaigne

OLDER AND WISER

OLD AGE IS LIKE A PLANE FLYING THROUGH A STORM. ONCE YOU'RE ABOARD, THERE'S NOTHING YOU CAN DO.

Golda Meir

If age imparted wisdom, there
wouldn't be any old fools.

Claudia Young

The person who is too
old to learn was probably
always too old to learn.

Caryl Haskins

As I get older, I get smaller.
I see other parts of the
world I didn't see before.

Neil Young

The more sand has escaped from
the hourglass of our life, the
clearer we should see through it.

Niccolò Machiavelli

To keep the heart unwrinkled,
to be hopeful, kindly,
cheerful, reverent – that is
to triumph over old age.

Thomas Bailey Aldrich

To know how to grow old is the
master work of wisdom, and
one of the most difficult chapters
in the great art of living.

Henri-Frédéric Amiel

FASCINATING FACT

Emeritus Professor Dr Heinz Wenderoth was the oldest person to ever receive a PhD at the age of 97 years and 8 months, when he received a Doctorate in Science from the University of Hannover.

I **NEVER** DARED BE
RADICAL WHEN **YOUNG**
FOR **FEAR** IT WOULD MAKE
ME **CONSERVATIVE**
WHEN **OLD.**

Robert Frost

They told me if I got older
I'd get wiser. In that case
I must be a genius.

George Burns

Experience is a terrible teacher
who sends horrific bills.

Anonymous

Old age is ready to undertake
tasks that youth shirked because
they would take too long.

W. Somerset Maugham

Age is opportunity no
less than youth itself.

Henry Wadsworth Longfellow

You don't get older, you get better.

Shirley Bassey

The elderly don't drive that badly;
they're just the only ones with
time to do the speed limit.

Jason Love

I've reached an age when I
can't use my youth as an excuse
for my ignorance any more.

Helen-Janet Bonellie

Don't just count your years,
make your years count.

Ernest Myers

We are not limited by our old
age; we are liberated by it.

Stu Mittleman

WHEN PEOPLE ARE OLD
ENOUGH TO KNOW
BETTER, THEY'RE OLD
ENOUGH TO DO WORSE.

Hesketh Pearson

A good head and a
good heart are always a
formidable combination.

Nelson Mandela

If nothing is going well,
call your grandmother.

Italian proverb

There's no fool like an old fool...
you can't beat experience.

Jacob Morton Braude

Learning sleeps and snores
in libraries, but wisdom
is everywhere, wide
awake, on tiptoes.

Josh Billings

The best part of the art of
living is to know how to
grow old gracefully.

Eric Hoffer

Experience is a comb that life
gives you after you lose your hair.

Judith Stern

FASCINATING FACT

Arthur Dake was a chess grandmaster and continued to play in rated tournaments until he passed away at the age of 89.

FROM **BIRTH** TO AGE 18, A **GIRL** NEEDS GOOD **PARENTS**... FROM 55 ON, SHE NEEDS **CASH.**

Sophie Tucker

He who devotes sixteen hours
a day to hard study may
become at 60 as wise as he
thought himself at 20.

Mary Wilson Little

Wrinkles should merely indicate
where smiles have been.

Mark Twain

We are young only once, after
that we need some other excuse.

Anonymous

If you don't learn to laugh at trouble, you won't have anything to laugh at when you're old.

Edgar Watson Howe

Be kind to your kids, they'll be choosing your nursing home.

Abraham Maslow

When you get to 52 food becomes more important than sex.

Prue Leith

FASCINATING FACT

In 2005, a study of over 400 pensioners found that cognitive ability is not a prime factor in achieving satisfaction in life. Although being smart is something that helps you get on well in life, when it comes to happiness in later years it's not such a big deal!

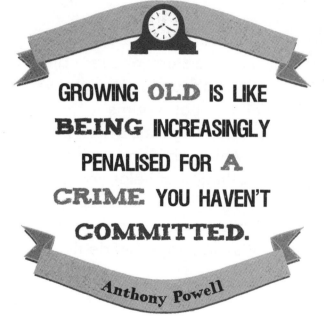

GROWING **OLD** IS LIKE **BEING** INCREASINGLY PENALISED FOR **A** **CRIME** YOU HAVEN'T **COMMITTED.**

Anthony Powell

Few people know how to be old.

François de la Rochefoucauld

A word to the wise ain't necessary – it's the stupid ones that need the advice.

Bill Cosby

One should never make one's debut in a scandal. One should reserve that to give interest to one's old age.

Oscar Wilde

I wouldn't like to die on stage. I'd settle for room service and a couple of dissipated women.

Peter O'Toole

A man is not old until his regrets take the place of dreams.

John Barrymore

I don't need you to remind me of my age, I have a bladder to do that for me.

Stephen Fry

FASCINATING FACT

The oldest person to receive a
Nobel Prize is Leonid Hurwicz,
who received the prize for
Economics in 2007 at the
age of 80. It's never too late
to make a difference!

If you young fellows were wise, the devil couldn't do anything to you, but since you aren't wise, you need us who are old.

Martin Luther

I'm 59 and people call me middle aged. How many 118-year-old men do you know?

Barry Cryer

You know you're getting old when you can pinch an inch on your forehead.

John Mendoza

LIFE'S
LITTLE
PLEASURES

MAYBE IT'S BECAUSE I'M GETTING OLDER... THE SIMPLE ACT OF TASTING A GLASS OF WINE IS ITS OWN EVENT.

David Hyde Pierce

If I had my life to live over again, I would make the same mistakes, only sooner.

Tallulah Bankhead

No matter what happens, I'm loud, noisy, earthy and ready for much more living.

Elizabeth Taylor

Passing the vodka bottle and playing the guitar.

Keith Richards on how he keeps fit

I'm like old wine. They don't
bring me out very often,
but I'm well preserved.

Rose Fitzgerald Kennedy

Water, taken in moderation,
cannot hurt anybody.

Mark Twain

I can still enjoy sex at 74. I live
at 75, so it's no distance.

Bob Monkhouse

FASCINATING FACT

At 92, John Lowe is Britain's oldest ballet dancer. In his life he has been a soldier in World War Two, an art teacher and a theatre director, but now dedicates his time to dance, to the point of even having installed a trapeze in his living room!

IT'S IMPORTANT TO HAVE A TWINKLE IN YOUR WRINKLE.

Anonymous

One of the best parts of growing older? You can flirt all you like since you've become harmless.

Liz Smith

How people keep correcting us when we are young! There is always some bad habit or other they tell us we ought to get over. Yet most bad habits are tools to help us through life.

Friedrich Nietzsche

With mirth and laughter let old wrinkles come.

William Shakespeare

If you give up smoking, drinking and loving, you don't actually live longer, it just seems longer.

Clement Freud

You are never too old to set another goal or to dream a new dream.

C. S. Lewis

Give me chastity and continence, but not yet.

St Augustine

It's sex, not youth, that's wasted on the young.

Janet Harris

My doctor told me to watch my drinking, so I now do it in front of the mirror.

Rodney Dangerfield

Most grandmas have a touch of the scallywag.

Helen Thomson

I'M **TOO OLD** TO DO THINGS **BY HALF.**

Lou Reed

The secret to staying young
is to live honestly, eat slowly,
and lie about your age.

Lucille Ball

I don't need drugs any more,
thank God. I can get the same
effect just by standing up real fast.

Jonathan Katz

I'd hate to die with a good liver,
good kidneys and a good brain...
I want everything to be knackered.

Hamish Imlach

If they don't have chocolate
in heaven I'm not going.

Roseanne Barr

Wine is a living liquid
containing no preservatives.

Julia Child

All decent people live beyond
their incomes nowadays, and
those who aren't respectable
live beyond other peoples'.

Saki

FASCINATING FACT

Dubbed 'grandad-olescents', an increasing number of retirees are choosing to forget about the bank balance and have a ball. A survey in 2008 noted that over a fifth of the 2,000 baby-boomers interviewed planned a long-haul round-the-world trip for their retirement, regardless of financial uncertainty.

THE **MORE** YOU PRAISE
AND **CELEBRATE**
YOUR **LIFE**, THE MORE
THERE IS IN LIFE TO
CELEBRATE.

Oprah Winfrey

The older one grows, the
more one likes indecency.

Virginia Woolf

Hatred of domestic work
is a natural and admirable
result of civilisation.

Rebecca West

I've never met a woman in my life
who would give up lunch for sex.

Erma Bombeck

If you obey all the rules,
you miss all the fun.

Katharine Hepburn

The lovely thing about being
40 is that you can appreciate
25-year-old men more.

Colleen McCullough

When I'm old and grey, I want
to have a house by the sea...
with a lot of wonderful chums,
good music and booze around.

Ava Gardner

FASCINATING FACT

Spicing things up in your later years is never out of the question. Just ask Dorothy Dale Kloss, 85, who is the world's oldest performing showgirl. She first performed in the 1930s and apparently taught Bob Fosse to dance.

THERE COMES A TIME
IN EVERY WOMAN'S
LIFE WHEN THE ONLY
THING THAT HELPS IS A
GLASS OF CHAMPAGNE.

Bette Davis

Seize the moment. Remember all those women on the Titanic who waved off the dessert cart.

Erma Bombeck

Anything worth doing is worth overdoing.

Mick Jagger

I'm limitless as far as age is concerned... as long as he has a driver's licence.

Kim Cattrall on dating younger men

A man is only as old as
the woman he feels.

Groucho Marx

There's a beauty to wisdom
and experience that cannot
be faked. It's impossible to be
mature without having lived.

Amy Grant

One of the many pleasures of
old age is giving things up.

Malcolm Muggeridge

FASCINATING FACT

For some, retirement – having the freedom to enjoy each day without the business of a regular occupation – can be daunting. But fear not! A study conducted in 2002 revealed that over half of those retirees interviewed were happier than they were before they hung up their guns.

Think big thoughts but
relish small pleasures.

H. Jackson Brown Jr

The aim of life is to live,
and to live means to be
aware, joyously, drunkenly,
serenely, divinely aware.

Henry Miller

I finally figured out the only
reason to be alive is to enjoy it.

Rita Mae Brown

WHEN IT COMES TO
STAYING YOUNG,
A MIND LIFT BEATS A
FACE LIFT ANY DAY.

Marty Bucella

Every time I think that I'm getting old, and gradually going to the grave, something else happens.

Elvis Presley

There are people whose watch stops at a certain hour and who remain permanently at that age.

Helen Rowland

Life may not be the party we hoped for, but while we're here we should dance.

Proverb

I think, therefore I still am.

Elliot Priest

Old age is like everything else. To make a success of it, you've got to start young.

Fred Astaire

I reckon responsible behaviour is something to get when you grow older. Like varicose veins.

Terry Pratchett

FASCINATING FACT

Christopher Lee, the actor
known for his roles as Dracula
for Hammer Horror and Saruman
in *The Lord of the Rings* trilogy,
made his debut as a heavy
metal vocalist at the age of 87,
with his concept album about
King Charlemagne, founder
of the Holy Roman Empire.

MY **HEROES** ARE
PEOPLE LIKE **PICASSO**
AND **MIRO** AND PEOPLE
WHO **AT LAST** REALLY
REACH **SOMETHING**
IN THEIR **OLD AGE.**

Robert Wyatt

I'm saving that rocker for the day
when I feel as old as I really am.

Dwight D. Eisenhower

Some people are born old
and tired while others are
going strong at 70.

Dorothy Thompson

You are only young once, but you
can be immature for a lifetime.

John P. Grier

If you rest, you rust.

Helen Hayes

We are always the
same age inside.

Gertrude Stein

Age should not have its face
lifted, but it should rather teach
the world to admire wrinkles
as the etchings of experience.

Clarence Day

In the midst of winter, I finally
learned that there was in
me an invincible summer.

Albert Camus

The older you get the more
important it is not to act your age.

Ashleigh Brilliant

Inside every older person is a
younger person – wondering
what the hell happened.

Cora Harvey Armstrong

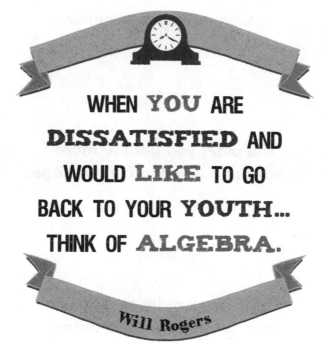

WHEN **YOU** ARE **DISSATISFIED** AND WOULD **LIKE** TO GO BACK TO YOUR **YOUTH**... THINK OF **ALGEBRA**.

Will Rogers

Like many women my age,
I am 28 years old.

Mary Schmich

The best tunes are played
on the oldest fiddles.

Ralph Waldo Emerson

I like my whisky old and
my women young.

Errol Flynn

You can't help getting older,
but you don't have to get old.

George Burns

Fifty is the new 34.

Emma Soames

It's too late for me to retire now.

Michael Caine at 70

FASCINATING FACT

A study by Swedish researchers in 2008 found that 68 per cent of married men in their 70s and 56 per cent of married women in their 70s were still having sex – still got it and still getting it!

TO **STOP** AGEING –
KEEP ON **RAGING.**

Dale Carnegie

Time and trouble will
tame an advanced young
woman, but an advanced
old woman is uncontrollable
by any earthly force.

Dorothy L. Sayers

When they tell me I'm
too old to do something, I
attempt it immediately.

Pablo Picasso

When people tell you how
young you look they are also
telling you how old you are.

Cary Grant

We are happier in many ways
when we are old than when
we were young. The young sow
wild oats. The old grow sage.

Winston Churchill

The ageing process has you
firmly in its grasp if you never get
the urge to throw a snowball.

Doug Larson

I'm surprised that I'm 50...
I still feel like a kid.

Bruce Willis

FASCINATING FACT

British pilot Peter Chantler broke the world record for the oldest person to make a solo helicopter flight when he flew for ten minutes over a farm in Chester at the age of 83.

YOU'RE **NEVER** TOO OLD
TO BECOME **YOUNGER**.

Mae West

Another belief of mine: that everyone else my age is an adult, whereas I am merely in disguise.

Margaret Atwood

There is no pleasure worth forgoing just for an extra three years in the geriatric ward.

John Mortimer

You can live to be a hundred if you give up all the things that make you want to.

Woody Allen

It is not by the grey of
the hair that one knows
the age of the heart.

Edward G. Bulwer-Lytton

Getting old ain't for sissies.

Bette Davis

Don't let ageing get you down.
It's too hard to get back up.

John Wagner

FASCINATING FACT

People in the over-sixties age group are most likely to find love abroad. What's more, almost ten per cent of holiday romances lead to wedding bells!

SUDDENLY SENIOR

The Funny Thing About Getting Older

Tom Hay

ISBN: 978-1-84953-076-7

Hardback

£9.99

You can't help feeling bewildered every time another birthday lunges at you – after all, you still feel like the proverbial spring chicken. And yet there are unmistakeable signs that seniority is creeping in. Don't worry, that's senior, not senile.

If you've ever had a senior moment, are afraid of acting your age or are positively deranged and confused, this miscellany of wit, jokes and quotations will remind you that age can be a funny old thing.

ODES FOR OLDIES

Clive Whichelow

ISBN: 978-1-84953-242-6
Hardback
£9.99

This collection of comical verse on all things oldie, from going grey to growing old disgracefully, is the perfect pick-me-up for those who have been there, done it and want to do it all over again!

If you're interested in finding out more about our humour books, follow us on Twitter: @SummersdaleLOL

www.summersdale.com